CHELSEA'S MAESTRO
A TRIBUTE TO GIANFRANCO ZOLA

Jerry Ewing

MAINSTREAM
PUBLISHING

EDINBURGH AND LONDON

First published in Great Britain in 1997 by
MAINSTREAM PUBLISHING COMPANY (EDINBURGH) LIMITED
7 Albany Street
Edinburgh EH1 3UG

ISBN 1 84018 045 5

A catalogue record for this book is available from the British Library

Designed by Ian McPherson

Printed and bound in Great Britain by The Bath Press Colourbooks, Glasgow

CHELSEA'S MAESTRO
A Tribute To Gianfranco Zola

Contents

AUTHOR'S ACKNOWLEDGEMENTS

Indebted thanks for all their help to: Kevin Whitcher, Adrian Finnis, Andrew Stearman, Andy Ryan, Dave Ling, Manure Ken, Malcolm Dome, Mick Wall, Shaun Hutson (Chelsea 4 Liverpool 2 and don't you forget it), Klunk and cheers to all the faithful down The Seven Stars

Also acknowledgements to the following publications which have proved invaluable source material: *Shoot, Match, Total Sport, 90 Minutes, World Soccer, Goal, Football Italia, Tutto Sport, The Sun, The Daily Telegraph, The Times Magazine, The Sunday Times, The Independent, The Daily Mail, The News Of The World, The Daily Mirror* and the *Evening Standard*

Zola Power

When Gianfranco Zola signed for Chelsea on November 8, 1996, few could have predicted the impact the little Italian would have on both Chelsea Football Club and English football as a whole.

Not so Ruud Gullit, the enigmatic Dutch wonder who signed the five-foot five-inch forward from Serie A club Parma for £4.5 million, adding the diminutive Italian to his squad of ever-increasing international expertise. Zola would feel even more at home when he joined his countrymen already housed at Stamford Bridge, Gianluca Vialli and Roberto Di Matteo.

"He is the sort of player who can decide a game with his vision, technique and ability to open it up from even ordinary situations," said the Blues' player-manager. "At Parma this season he has been a victim of a change in the playing style. If Parma didn't want to use his quality I knew I'd like to have it."

Carlo Ancelotti, the Parma manager who brought in Croatian Mario Stanic to play in the role that Zola was used to and precipitated the forward's departure to London's Fulham Road, would have been more than aware too, that such an ill-advised move could return to haunt him as "Fonzie" (as his new Chelsea team mates would quickly nickname him) turned on the Italian style in the English Premiership. Parma fans were disgruntled to say the least over the transfer. One-nil to Ruud Gullit.

A sight Chelsea fans would soon get used to: Zola celebrates the second of his goals against Wimbledon

Glenn Hoddle, England's new coach, had once tried to sign Zola during his own managerial stint at Chelsea, only to be put off by a price quoted as £10 million. Later in the season, Hoddle's admiration for Zola would return to haunt him, too.

Gianfranco Zola had been wowing UK football fans and the massed ranks of the footballing press with his Premiership antics for a mere four months before his quite astonishing footballing skills hit the headlines in the manner that many in the English game had begun to fear in the build-up to England's World Cup qualifying match with Italy at Wembley on February 12. As one paper put it: "Tell Gianfranco Zola that he is regarded as Italy's talisman at

Wembley in 10 days time and that boyish face breaks out into a shy, toothy grin.

"I am very fulfilled at Chelsea," he says. "I am loving my football and these are the right conditions for me to give of my best."

It is the deepest of paradoxes for England's coach Glenn Hoddle that here, nestling in the club where he cut his teeth as a Premiership Manager, is the man who might drag the World Cup rug from beneath him."

Germany and penalty shoot-outs notwithstanding, the Italian national team has long been a thorn in our side. In 1978, A 2—0 loss for England in Italy meant that reaching the Finals in Argentina was beyond us. Not even a 2—0 victory on home soil could diffuse the blow to national pride, and the felling of goalscorer (and at the time national hero) Kevin Keegan by Marco Tardelli, a move in keeping with the then vicious nature of Italian football at the time, merely rubbed salt into a particularly nasty wound.

This was the ground on which the press, full of their usual national fervour, built up the qualifier between the two countries. Hoddle's side were unbeaten going into the game, and despite the odd drearily unfulfilled performance that English football fans have become accustomed to, the team were showing definite promise. The vision of free-flowing play that Hoddle had begun to struvture at Chelsea was slowly beginning to make its mark at international level.

Zola, already enjoying the open play at Chelsea that Hoddle had begun and Gullit ahd continued to encourage, felt Wembley would be to his liking. He loves the big stage, and always feels he can pull out his best on it.

"I cannotnot wait to go dancing across the wide open spaces of Wembley," he said, ominously, during the build-up to the game.

The warning signs had been all too evident when the footballing dynamo had destroyed Northern Ireland in a friendly game earlier in the year, scoring one goal and creating a string of chances, to the obvious admiration of the new Italian national coach Cesare Maldini.

Come the night of February 12, Zola worked his magic. A decisive long ball out of the Italian defence by Costacurta was seized upon by the little Sardinian after the usually dependable Stuart Pearce was caught napping on the right hand side of the field. Heading towards goal like a greyhound after a hare, Zola skipped past Sol Campbell. Just as the crowd seemed to breathe a collective sigh of relief as it seemed that the Chelsea man had pushed the ball just a touch too far ahead of him, he swept it in with a punishing strike that rocketed past Ian Walker in goal, beating the 'keeper at his near post. And that was that. Italy closed up, England failed to find the breakthrough and Hoddle's first defeat placed the nation's World Cup dreams in jeopardy. Thanks once more to Italy. And Gianfranco Zola in particular.

"I'm sorry" was Franco's response to the British press on what has constantly been referred to as "THAT goal". The fact that Zola didn't have what could be considered a particularly outstanding game, says more about the impact that this particular Italian import has had on the UK's football scene, and the acclaim that he has received.

"You have to understand it is my job," said Zola by way of explanation, whilst his own countrymen rejoiced, basking in the warm glow of such an important victory. "But I'm sorry for England because this is my second home where I have been made to feel so welcome."

It was a typical response from the Italian, displaying his

Zola has both delighted and haunted English fans

customary courtesy and humility. He had some words of comfort, too.

"I think England will qualify, though. And I hope they do because England is one of the most important countries in football. I cannot think of a World Cup without England, or without Italy, Germany or Brazil. These are the main countries in the whole world of football, the teams people from all around the world are interested in."

"If the European Championships were decided on charm, this little man would already be carrying off his gold medal," said Football Italia's Editor John D Taylor prior to the Euro 96 tournament, going on to refer to Gianfranco as "the genuine article - shy, modest and unassuming."

Shy and modest Zola's style of play most certainly isn't. But his introduction to international football was certainly veering towards the unassuming. Zola didn't appear in an Italian shirt until he was 25 years old, by which time he'd already played for Nuorese, Torres and Napoli. A classic late developer, he didn't notch his first for Italy until almost four years later, slotting home in a 4–1 victory against Estonia.

Italian coach Cesare Maldini congratulates Zola, his tiny destroyer

In fact, Zola's first taste of the English game in which he now commands such a starring role came even before he'd been picked for the Italian national team. Whilst holidaying in his native Sardinia in the summer of 1990, the 24-year-old Gianfranco was playing in the Napoli reserve team when a surprise telephone call offered him a chance to play for a local side against Bobby Robson's England team, who had set up training camp for the Italian 1990 World Cup finals on the small island. In a game in which the local team (mostly made up of fishermen and farmers) were to lose 10–2, Zola found himself up against the likes of David

Seaman, Mark Wright, Peter Beardsley and hardman Steve McMahon.

"It was the first time I had ever played English players and it was 10–2. It was desperate!" Gianfranco remembers. "I was the only professional in our team, the rest were all amateurs. England had their full side out at one stage. It was just a warm-up game for them. For me it was a great experience. I had only read about these guys before that game."

Yet somewhat surprisingly for a player whose game is today flourishing in a way which belies his 30 years, Zola's

Hours of practice have made Gianfranco deadly with the dead-ball

early international career had been better known for two distinct blots. Having spent much of the 1994 World Cup in the USA warming up the bench, Zola was introduced into a game against Nigeria as substitute. The game was a bad-tempered affair, which saw the Mexican referee Arturo Brizio rapidly lose control, but nonetheless it still seems amazing that the mild-mannered Zola was sent off after barely 15 minutes. He appealed, claiming the dismissal was unjust, but FIFA secretary Sepp Blatter decreed the sending off perfectly fair. Gianfranco missed the rest of the tournament.

And perhaps more fresh in the memory is his performance in Euro 96. Despite a scintillating display against Russia in which he set up Casiraghi for a stunning strike, it was his penalty miss against Germany which many remember him for. Casiraghi had been tripped in the German box within the first 10 minutes and it was Zola who stepped up to the spot in front of the Kop at Anfield.

His penalty was weakly-struck and the German 'keeper

Kopke dived low to turn the ball round the left-hand post. The game finished a 0—0 draw and Italy were on their way home. Their failure ultimately cost coach Arrigo Sacchi his job.

It takes a brave man to turn things around in such a short space of time. With his strike at Wembley, Zola was hailed in his homeland as a true match-winner, a player who can turn a match in a moment. The little man who came late to the game had the experience and spirit to come back from adversity.

Last season brought perhaps his biggest challenges and greatest triumphs. As he pushed Italy towards France 98, he took a Chelsea side of emerging potential and rewarded them with genuine success and hope of a bright new era.

The likes of Liverpool, Manchester United, Wimbledon, West Ham and Middlesbrough suffered at his oh-so talented feet. And Chelsea Football Club, the much berated sleeping giant of so many years, achieved glory once more. He is truly a remarkable character.

Blue Is The Colour

Ruud Gullit's arrival at Stamford Bridge in the summer of 1995 was as much of a shock to Chelsea fans as it was to the rest of the Chelsea team. Here was a player who had been regarded, quite rightly, as the best in the world, and there is little in the world of football that hasn't been achieved by this truly remarkable character.

He has played with some of the world's top football clubs; a list that includes Feyenoord, PSV Eindhoven, AC Milan and Sampdoria. He has appeared in the 1990 World Cup Finals, and in two European Championships, leading the Dutch national team to victory in one final against Russia, in which he scored one of the goals. He helped Milan to three Serie A championships (1988, 1992 and 1993) and two consecutive European Cup Final victories in 1989 and 1990. Add both European Footballer of the Year and World Footballer of the Year titles and here you have a footballing enigma. So what on earth is he doing at Chelsea, some may have wondered.

Gullit arrived at Stamford Bridge in a blaze of publicity, a major coup for the manager Glenn Hoddle, and perhaps one of the first signings of his managerial career that suggested that his vision of the beautiful game was attracting the kind of players required to fulfil the manager's goals. Immediately he stood like a colossus on the pitch, both metaphorically as well as physically (alongside one of the shortest teams in the Premiership), and his presence went some way to settling a team well known for its lack of consistency. He quickly struck up a friendship and understanding with another surprise signing, Mark Hughes, who arrived a month after him. Once more Stamford Bridge buzzed with the hum of expectancy. Only this time there seemed to be a feeling that expectancy really would bear fruit. That it ended with a mid-table position and losing to Manchester United in the semi-finals of the FA Cup gave no indication of what was to follow.

In action for the Azzuri

Chelsea's lack of major silverware in a history that has always seen the club amongst the cream of the country's footballing sides has long been a cross born by fans and players alike. Regarded as one of the most glamorous clubs this country has produced, it has always been to Dave Sexton's team of the Seventies that Chelsea have fans looked. To the team that included Stamford Bridge heroes like Peter Osgood, Peter Bonetti, Eddie McCreadie, Charlie Cooke, Alan Hudson, Dave Webb and Ron Harris. It was this team that best encapsulates the Stamford Bridge glory days, days that Chelsea fans have hankered after ever since.

Chelsea's first and only League Championship came in the 1954–5 season, under the managership of Ted Drake.

The wait for further glory lasted 10 years, until the club lifted the League Cup in 1965. Five years later and it seemed that the promise of all those years was coming to fruition. Chelsea famously defeated favourites Leeds United 2–1 to win the FA Cup in 1970 in a replay at Old Trafford (having drawn at Wembley 2–2). A year later they would go on to lift the European Cup Winners Cup, defeating Spaniards Real Madrid 2–1 (after another 1–1 draw). The halcyon days had seemingly arrived. Or had they?

No sooner had it seemed that Chelsea were on their destined path to glory and acclaim, they suddenly seemed to allow everything to slip out from underneath them. They reached the League Cup Final again in 1972 only to lose to highly unfancied Stoke City 2–1. And despite racking up their highest ever score in the first round of the 1971–2 European Cup Winners Cup with a 13–0 home drubbing of Luxembourg side Juenesse Hautcharage which included five goals from the heroic Peter Osgood (an 8–0 away leg victory gave them a record 21–0 aggregate score), they would go out in the second round to Swedish side Advitaberg on the away goals rule. From thereonin it was downhill all the way.

Expansive ground development plans landed the club with crippling financial debts. Expansive, that is, for the

Zola sails past Sol Campbell to score for Italy against England at Wembley

Zola in jokey mood with a bowler hat as he prepared to leave Italy and become an honorary Londoner

time, and nothing compared to the delightful development that Stamford Bridge has currently undergone. In reality all it amounted to was the building of the overpowering (and overbearing) East Stand, nicknamed 'The Vertigo Stand' by fans owing to its user unfriendliness, but it was still enough to see many of the clubs best players sold off to help ease the financial burden. Dave Sexton was off to West London neighbours Queens Park Rangers in 1974, thus beginning a run of a series of some 11 managers in a 20 year period. Relegation battles became the norm, and the team that

once encapsulated the glamour of nearby Kings Road found themselves enduring two stints in Division Two (Chelsea achieving a magnificent 94 goals and 99 points when they won the Second Division Championship in 1989).

When Chairman Ken Bates arrived in 1982, reputedly buying the club from the stricken Mears family (H.A. Mears had originally built the ground at the turn of the century without a team and even offered it to nearby Fulham at one stage) for just one pound, Chelsea were in turmoil. A team that could finish in the top six of Division One one season

Gianfranco takes off Robin Hood as he prepares to become an English hero himself!

Gianfranco gets to grips with Faustino Asprilla during their time together at Parma

could end up being relegated the next. A host of quality players began their careers at Stamford Bridge, only to find themselves reaping real rewards at other clubs, names like Wilkins, Dorigo, Le Saux, Townsend and Durie. Others, like Langley, Finnieston, Walker and Fleck never seemed to fulfil their potential, and a policy of buying players in the autumn of their careers saw the likes of Bryan 'Pop' Robson, Colin Viljoen, Duncan McKenzie, Mick Harford and Clive Allen all spend time at the Bridge. Appearances in Cup competitions like the Full Members Cup (which Chelsea won in 1986) and the Zenith Data Systems Cup (winners in 1990) and Bates' difficult relationship with the press didn't help. Chelsea were not being taken seriously.

Glenn Hoddle first arrived at Stamford Bridge from French side Monaco in the early Nineties to train after injury threatened to kill of his glorious career. Although he didn't turn out for the first team, he did play a couple of games for Chelsea reserves, before heading off to manage Second Division Swindon Town. Whether he was sent there by the London Club in order to groom him for his later stint as Player/Manager has never been established, but after Ian Porterfield's disastrous run between 1991 and 1993, and David Webb's short-holding tenure, Hoddle returned to the club in time for the 1994–5 season. Expectations ran high.

Despite his expertise and vision of how the game should be played, Hoddle's luck in the league was plagued by inconsistency on the pitch. And despite such a high profile career as a player (arguably the closest answer to Ruud Gullit this country has seen), his player buying policy seemed to lack experience (Andy Dow, David Rocastle, Paul Furlong, Mark Stein). However, despite three seasons of mid-table obscurity, in his first season at the helm Glenn Hoddle took Chelsea to their first FA Cup Final for 24 years. They learnt a cruel lesson as Manchester United destroyed them 4–0. The inexperience on the big stage all too evident in the likes of Frank Sinclair and Eddie Newton. Two penalties, one highly debatable, left referee of the day David Elleray forever on the hate list of the Chelsea faithful. And it was Mark Hughes who slotted home goal number four!

Hoddle believed that Chelsea could learn from the experience, and a year later he steered Chelsea to the semi-finals of the European Cup Winners Cup, before they fell to a Real Zaragoza side inspired by Uruguayan international Gustavo Poyet and who would eventually win the Cup. However, it was Hoddle's final year at Stamford Bridge before he was wrested away by the FA to take charge of the national team, that proved the most important in Chelsea's recent history.

Face in the crowd: Gianfranco
snaps some pictures of his
new surroundings

Zola takes a spectacular tumble as the ref prepares to blow up for a foul

Ruud Gullit's arrival came after a blaze of publicity suggesting Chelsea were after Paul Gascoigne, proving that the club really were prepared to put their money where their mouths were. The arrival on the scene of Matthew Harding, the head of the Benfield Insurance Group and massive Chelsea fan, saw a much needed cash injection, and although Gullit arrived from Sampdoria on a free transfer, there was a two year contract worth a reported £2 million to take into account. The subsequent arrival of Mark Hughes from Manchester United proved an even bigger shock (to fans of both clubs, but to the obvious delight of Chelsea), and the capture of Romanian international Dan Petrescu from Sheffield Wednesday proved an astute purchase and really showed that Chelsea meant business. The disappointment of losing to arch rivals Manchester United in the semi-finals of the FA Cup and the loss of Hoddle as Manager didn't dampen the enthusiasm of fans and players alike. Mark Hughes, so often the subject of transfer talk aimed at unsettling the player into leaving remained, despite an unspectacular first season at the club. And when Ruud Gullit was appointed player-manager to the delight of fans

who had left no doubt as to who it was they wanted to succeed Hoddle (horrified no doubt, by press reports that George Graham and his negative approach would be installed, ruining Hoddle's good work), the expectancy returned. The sleeping giant was awakening this time, wasn't he?

For a man that has achieved so much in his distinguished career, Gullit's approach has always been laid back. A graceful yet immensely strong player, even when on the pitch a sudden burst of speed can seem as relaxed as it is intense. And thus his managerial approach has been an intriguing blend of casual and solidly professional. Gone, for example, was the nickname "Big Nose" foisted upon him by Dennis Wise (who else?).

"That came about from when he was a player," remarked defender Steve Clarke. "We all call him boss now."

With the Bosman Ruling now meaning that out of contract foreign players could move clubs with no transfer fee, and with English clubs continuing to demand ludicrous transfer fees Gullit set about using his own pulling power, dipping into the Italian Serie A to snatch first Gianluca

Up and over:
Gianfranco
hurdles a high
challenge

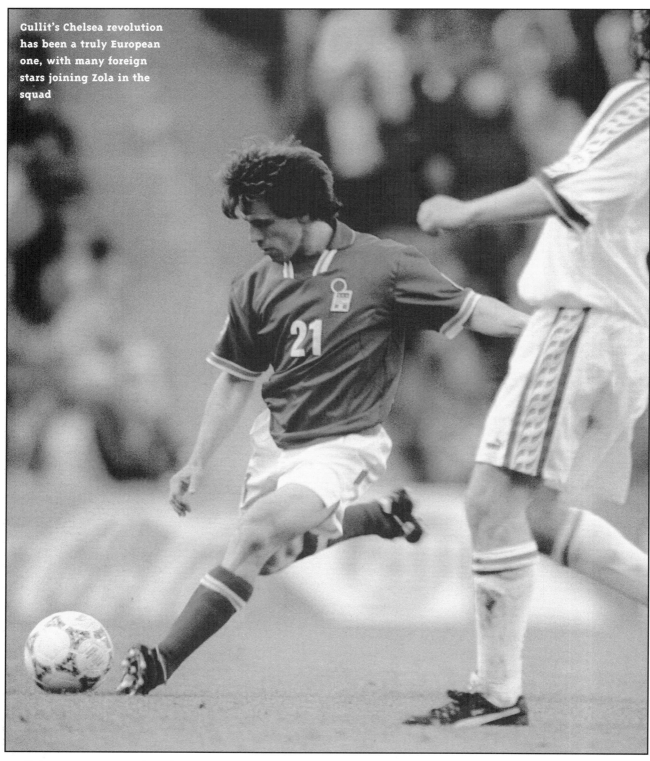

Gullit's Chelsea revolution has been a truly European one, with many foreign stars joining Zola in the squad

Vialli from Juventus on a free, then Roberto Di Matteo from Lazio for £4.9 million, before switching to Strasbourg to acquire French defender Frank Lebouef for £2.5 million. The name Chelsea was becoming synonymous with the old Kings Road swagger once more, only in keeping with the ways of modern football it was laced with a European flavour. And it was the arrival in November 1996 of Gianfranco Zola from Parma that suggested not only had

Gullit settled quickly into his new role, but both he and the club were aware of what it was that Chelsea needed to help them maintain that top flight run that had so long eluded them. The beginning of a revolution at Stamford Bridge that many had hoped for and few thought they really would see.

And a revolution in which little Gianfranco Zola would play a starring role.

Zola warms up
those magic
boots

Zola's arrival was to
transform the fortunes
at Stamford Bridge

His Name Is Zola

"I think with Gianfranco that his abilities are obvious. He has great technical ability and he sees the game very well."

These were the words with which Chelsea player-manager Ruud Gullit welcomed Italian Gianfranco Zola into his new look Chelsea side. Words which would have a prophetic ring about them within weeks.

"You don't get an opportunity like this every day and when I heard he might be available I knew I wanted him to come to Chelsea," continued the dreadlocked Dutchman.

Born on May 7, 1966 in Oliena (where his father Ignazio owned a bar) on the Island of Sardinia, which lies to the west of the boot-shaped strip of mainland, Zola's home-

town has been referred to as a "footballing backwater", a place where the scouts who eagerly hunt for the voracious talents of young would-be Italian footballers rarely ventured. Serie A club Cagliari is one of the few Sardinian clubs to make any kind of headlines around the world.

At a mere 5 feet 5 inches high, and at just 65kg, the diminutive Sardinian would need to rely on sheer skill and talent to make any headway in the fanatical world of Italian football. Anyone who's seen him play for Chelsea will, however, know that this flows in abundance.

He joined Nuoerese in 1983, at the age of 17. He would turn out 31 times over the three year stint, and score 10 goals with the little Italian club, who were in C2 (roughly

Premiership defences soon found they had to stop Zola any way they could...

the equivalent of our third division), but who were relegated to the International League in Zola's first season. In 1986, he moved back to C2 with Torres, another Sardinian team, for whom he racked up 88 appearances and scored 21 goals over another three year run.

"I never got the chance to play for Cagliari, the biggest team in Sardinia," reflects Zola on his early days.

It hardly mattered however, for during his time with Torres, Zola so impressed the club's Sports Director Nello Barbanera that he contacted Luciano Moggi, then general manager of Napoli, the Serie A club (he's now with Juventus) and a noted mover in the Italian football world. Despite Zola being pretty much an unknown quantity in the top rung of Italian football, Moggi was impressed enough to sign Zola for a sum that has been reported as being between £100,000 and £200,000.

It was here that the then 23-year-old came under the tutelage of Diego Maradona, the Argentine superstar who was also with Napoli at the time. And despite living in the

now disgraced footballer's shadow, Zola's undoubted skills impressed the Neopolitans, who dubbed him "Marazola".

"Zola, so good he looked like Maradona" stated Italy's footballing paper Gazzetta dello Sport after Zola had scored a 30 yard scorcher in a 3—1 win over Atalanta.

Zola and Maradona were only together for one season at Napoli, and many of the Sardinian's appearances for the team in his first season were as substitute for the maestro.

"Maradona changed my life," recalls Zola of the partnership. "He's the most inspiring player I have ever had the privilege of playing with. When he gave me his shirt one time, the famous No 10 light blue shirt, I was over the moon. I respected and loved Maradona very much, but I never felt scared of stepping into his shoes. I just thought 'I'm here to do a job and that job is to play football. I'll go out on the pitch and give my all'. That's all there is to it, as far as I'm concerned. End of story."

End of story and all there may be to it perhaps, but as any Chelsea fan will tell you, it's a philosophy that still dri-

The passion of the Italian fans equipped Zola well for the intense atmosphere of the Bridge

Three Italian stars set for England: Roberto Di Matteo, Gianfranco Zola and Fabrizio Ravanelli

ves the enigmatic Zola on to this day. It also helped Zola drive Napoli towards a European trophy and Zola's sole Italian Championship, before the club's financial situation forced them to sell the Sardinian to Parma, for whom he scored 62 goals in 140 appearances over a three year stint.

From almost humble footballing beginnings, Zola was now a player on the world stage. He had already racked up

his first appearance for Italy under Arrigo Saachi (always unappreciative of the creative genius he had in Zola) in a game against Norway. However, it wasn't until Cesare Maldini, father of Italian footballing icon Paulo and he of daftest hair in world football title, came to the fore after Saachi's arrogance and ignorance for the finer details of the Italian game (things like flair, artistic creativity and a

More hugs from
Maldini en-route to
France 98

After coming to stardom
late, Zola works hard on
maintaining his skills

Zola signed for Chelsea on November 8, 1996 and proved an immediate hit

view of the game nigh on unsurpassable) proved his undoing, that Zola began to achieve the kind of acclaim he so deserved. Acclaim that would attract the attention of then Chelsea boss Glenn Hoddle, who would unsuccessfully try to sign the little dynamo, and then Ruud Gullit, who, as with so much of his career, was successful in the capture of Gianfranco Zola.

And so it was that on Friday November 8, 1996, that Zola signed to Chelsea Football Club for £4.5 million, completing a triumvirate of Italian's offering new hope at Stamford Bridge. Gianluca Vialli, the ex-Juventus captain who had just won the Italian Cup and was steeped in Italian footballing folklore. Roberto Di Matteo, little known in this country when signed from Lazio, now the man with whom rests the glorious honour of not only scoring perhaps the greatest goal in an FA Cup Final, but also the quickest too. His £4.9 million fee now looks like a real bargain. And Gianfranco Zola, the man who many thought too physically small to take on the rigours of Premiership Football. The thought had even crossed Zola's own mind after that 1990 meeting with the England Squad, that saw Zola pitched against the towering figure of Arsenal's Tony Adams.

Zola brushed aside doubts that he'd be too small for the hurly-burly of the Premiership

"At first I thought I would be too small for English soccer," he said. "Adams didn't even have to jump to win the ball. It was a joke. I thought it would be the same for me if I came to England, that all defenders would be like that and I would have no chance. But I have grown since then in more ways than one. I am a better player. I have more variety in my game."

Zola joined a Chelsea team that had got off to a flying start to the new season, suggesting that Gullit's expertise and understanding of the game had already had a major impact, despite a drab opening match against perennial Premiership strugglers Southampton at The Dell which saw little to offer any excitement in the new arrivals. Yet Leboeuf and Vialli had found the net frequently in the opening exchanges of the season, and Gullit had tasted triumph almost immediately when the London side were victorious in the Umbro International tournament prior to the start of the season.

Celebration time for
the Bridge faithful

Zola's combination of
deception, pace and
mental agility keeps
him ahead

Success in Italy gave Zola the experience he needed when the going got tough for Chelsea

A six match unbeaten run, including victories against fellow import-laden Middlesborough and then league leaders Sheffield Wednesday, and a truly exciting 3–3 draw against North London rivals Arsenal at Highbury suggested hope for the Stamford Bridge side, even if cynics were tempted to suggest that the team may have shot their bolt too early. However a visit to Anfield saw Chelsea crash back to earth with a mighty bump. Liverpool destroyed Chelsea 5–1, giving rise to suggestions that the new arrivals "didn't like it up them" (Vialli's own petulant display being a prime factor), and also that the homegrown players still weren't up to it (Myers' disastrous own goal being a major offender).

There then followed a typical run of up and down Chelsea performances that saw a home defeat at the hands of Wimbledon which really showed a battered Frank Leboeuf what life in English football was all about, and lacklustre drawers against Aston Villa and Nottingham Forest off-set by a strident 2–1 victory at Old Trafford, going some way to making up for the misery of the FA Cup semi-final defeat the year before, and proving yet again that Chelsea remain Manchester United's prime jinx team.

Chelsea overcame a patchy start as the new arrivals got to know each other

In the meantime, however, tragedy had struck Chelsea on the night of October 22, when Club Director and financial benefactor (not to say major fan and fans' friend) Matthew Harding died in a helicopter crash following Chelsea being knocked out of the Coca-Cola Cup at Bolton. Harding, who had risen from tea boy to owning the Benfield Insurance Group, had been a life-long fan of the club, and when Ken Bates invited him to invest in Chelsea many fans felt that his cash injections, which paid for much of the on-going ground development and the influx of major players, was the lifeline that Chelsea had been waiting for. Despite waging a bitter war for control of the club with the bullish Bates in the pages of the tabloids, Harding was loved by players and fans alike, and his death was a major loss to Chelsea Football Club and the game itself.

The game following Harding's untimely demise was a home match against Tottenham Hotspur on October 26th. As Chelsea and Spurs players linked hands in the centre-circle a minute's silence was held around the country. For some, like Chelsea goalkeeper Kevin Hitchcock, it was almost too much to bear. Chelsea ran out 3–1 winners on the day (hardly a surprising result given the Blues' mastery of the North London club over the years) and the victory was immediately dedicated to the memory of Harding, with

both Gullit and Chelsea skipper Dennis Wise offering promises of winning a major trophy in memory of the late financial wizard. With the team out of one cup, the chances of silverware were becoming slimmer.

This was the scene that greeted the arrival of Gianfranco Zola at Stamford Bridge. Chelsea had not dropped out of the top half of the league, and despite some fine performances and some flowing football, they were still prone to too many defensive gaffes (shame on you Myers and Frank Sinclair) to successfully sustain a challenge to the likes of Manchester United, Liverpool and Newcastle. Zola, it was felt, could be the catalyst to change things.

"If Chelsea want to win the league, I want to be part of that," said the new arrival. "I certainly think that this team will be in Europe next season and perhaps even better than that. We are fifth now and I am sure we can progress from there."

Zola was thrown into the Premiership fray almost immediately, when Chelsea faced Blackburn Rovers at Ewood Park 10 days after his signing. The game ended a 1–1 draw, with Dan Petrescu scoring for the Blues, but the delightedly vociferous Chelsea support saw enough from the little Italian import to allow themselves an understanding of what was to come.

Zola's expertise in dead-ball situations opened up many new avenues for Chelsea's attacking play

Although one of Roberto Di Matteo's increasing number of long range strikes (what could he have been practising for?) was the first sign of Italian class, although Blackburn took the lead through Kevin Gallacher who neatly flicked the ball past Chelsea's Norwegian goalkeeper Frode Grodas (joining Zola as debutee), and although Petrescu levelled for the London side, it was two flashes of Zola power that hinted at what a buy this player had been.

The little Italian with the reputation for his ability to curl in a long range ball saw one effort from the edge of the area just fly over the upright with Tim Flowers stranded. And the renowned free-kick expert sent in a gloriously neat chip that Craig Burley sent just wide of the goal. One a chance from nowhere. The other, deft usage of the dead ball situation. Both splendid efforts from a man making his entrance into the English game.

Zola congratulates his
team-mate and compatriot
Roberto Di Matteo

Chelsea had a kit crisis away at Coventry — and ended up playing in the home side's away shirts!

The Blues Brothers

"The way he puts the ball on to your feet is unbelievable. And he can change the course of a game with just one touch of invention. Skill? He makes me look positively ordinary."

These were the words uttered by Gianluca Vialli when his fellow countryman Gianfranco Zola joined Chelsea from Parma. Words that would later return to haunt the ex-Juventus star as he would find himself languishing on the Chelsea substitutes bench.

Chelsea's start to the 1996—7 season had been impressive. Some had expressed doubt that Ruud Gullit would be able to handle the rigours of management in the Premiership at his first attempt. The ever-cool Dutchman proved them wrong. Seemingly taking everything in his stride, he refused to become phased by the hurly burly world of English soccer, and his grace as a player from the season previous was extended to his new level. The casual manner in which he conducted all pre and post match interviews was at odds to the terse commentary one would expect from Alex Ferguson or Kenny Dalglish, or the impassioned outbreaks from Kevin Keegan, and it remains a joy to hear. The bonhomie struck up with his fellow BBC commentators always makes for good viewing, and no Chelsea fan will ever forget Gullit, the player, taking on the expertise of Sky TV's Andy Gray in a compelling debate about the modern game and its tactics.

On the turn
for Chelsea

Arms outstretched towards the fans as he celebrates another super strike

More than aware of the situation of foreign players in Europe, and of his own standing amongst them, Gullit, much like Hoddle before him (as far as Gullit, Hughes and Petrescu were concerned), used his pulling power to lure some of Europe's finest players to Stamford Bridge, to the amazed delight of the Chelsea fans, and the first of these was Gianluca Vialli. A respected Italian international with 59 caps, Gullit captured Vialli within a week of him leading Juventus to the Italian Cup on a free transfer.

"Vialli has star quality," said Terry Venables of the new Stamford Bridge man. "He's like Eric Cantona. Those around him get an extra buzz."

A noted prankster (not to mention son of a millionaire who was brought up in a castle!), Vialli once, when playing for Sampdoria, famously filled team mate Graeme Souness' shoes with shaving foam and chopped the legs off of one of his suits. A brave man... He even filled Italian coach Arrigo Sacchi's napkin with Parmesan cheese at a team dinner, ruining his suit when he opened it. Needless to say, after that Vialli's days in the national squad were numbered.

All eyes were, of course, on Vialli as Chelsea mounted their new Premiership charge. Playing up front alongside Mark Hughes, Vialli's high work-rate and desire to have a crack at goal whenever the chance arose was evident from the off. At Southampton on the first day of the new season a tasty overhead effort almost secured Vialli his first Chelsea goal. As it was, he only had to wait until Chelsea's second home game, against Coventry, for that to arrive. When it did, it was a blistering strike into the back of the net, leaving Steve Ogrizovic with absolutely no chance whatsoever. Vialli, clearly delighted at making his mark, stormed to the Stamford Bridge West Stand in celebration.

Five more goals followed before the arrival of Gianfranco Zola, including one brilliant effort at Old Trafford nutmegging Manchester United keeper Peter Schmeichel in Chelsea's 2–1 victory. Few strikers can lay claim to such a boast. Vialli was scoring goals. But was he adapting to life in the Premiership with confident ease?

As for Mark Hughes, the man-mountain of a forward who had been captured from Manchester United when Glenn Hoddle discovered the Welshman and long-time Chelsea

Steve Clarke, a man who's seen many changes at the Bridge, congratulates Zola

fan had not in fact re-signed his United contract, it was a slightly different story. As the cry "Who the •••• are Man Utd" went up at Stamford Bridge on Hughes' first appearance at the West London ground, in a pre-season friendly against Porto, Hughes acknowledged the cry by cupping his ears and motioning to the crowd, ingratiating himself forever with fans who a season previous had detested the very ground he'd walked on for past footballing crimes against their beloved team. But Hughes was never a prolific goalscorer, and despite some glorious goals for Chelsea (in the Porto game he headed home in spectacular fashion), his first season was a quiet one. A tireless and frequently uncelebrated worker for the team, Hughes' start to the new season was also quiet, his first goal not coming until the season was nine games old.

From day one at Stamford Bridge Hughes' position was frequently under question. From the press, from United fans angered by his departure, and by those clubs jealous at Chelsea's capture of the noted footballing hardman. Never, though, Chelsea Football Club, Ruud Gullit, Ken Bates or Mark Hughes himself. How many times have Chelsea fans read in the tabloids of Hughes' imminent departure to Bolton or Everton, of his dislike of life down South, of his wife wanting to return back up North, where Hughes had his own house built. A quiet, private and intense individual, Hughes' polite denials never seemed enough to quell the rumours. Even after Chelsea's FA Cup Victory this season the rumours were still persisting that, with his family returned to the Cheshire home, he was off. Again, no substance and Hughes remains a Chelsea player

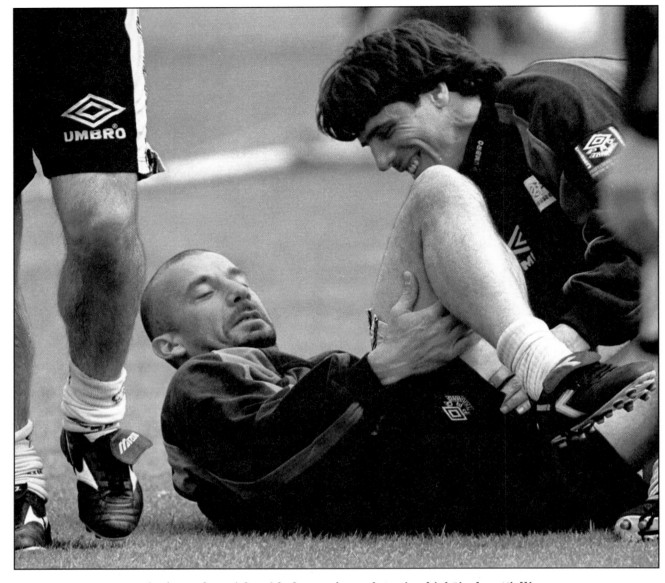

Gianfranco has a joke with the team's prankster-in-chief Gianluca Vialli

with a new contract. It'd be a daft club to allow a player of Hughes' magnitude to depart.

The arrival of Gianfranco Zola into the Chelsea frontline that also featured John Spencer and Mark Stein, only helped spark more rumours of Hughes' departure.

"Nobody has to go," answered Gullit. "If you look at our last few games Mark Hughes has been outstanding, a great help to the team. What's better for him is that he's been playing with better players and finding that fun and now we've got even more better players with Gianfranco here."

Indeed it was John Spencer who would be first to go. Although popular with the crowd and an asset to the team, Spencer couldn't live with the European style squad system Gullit was instigating, and his mouth let everyone know it. He now plays for QPR.

The original idea had been to play Zola just behind a front two of Hughes and Vialli (which in turn sparked the exit of Gavin Peacock, also to QPR). But Vialli and Hughes had failed to gel in the manner hoped for. That they were too alike as players had not gone unnoticed by the terrace commentators. Then fate played its trump card. Shortly after Zola arrived, Vialli was injured and Gullit pushed him into the attack alongside Hughes in a move which would really turn around the fortunes of a team still viewed as the "nearly men" by cynics.

Within one month Zola had been chosen as Carling's Player Of The Month, a mere indication of what he would achieve over the coming seven months. In the 3–1 against West Ham, he and Hughes were formidable, Hughes bagging two goals and Zola scoring one of the goals of the season (he would add another three over the Christmas period).

"Winning this award is a big surprise for me because I didn't think I'd done that well," announced Zola with

Zola and Vialli soak up
the Wembley atmosphere

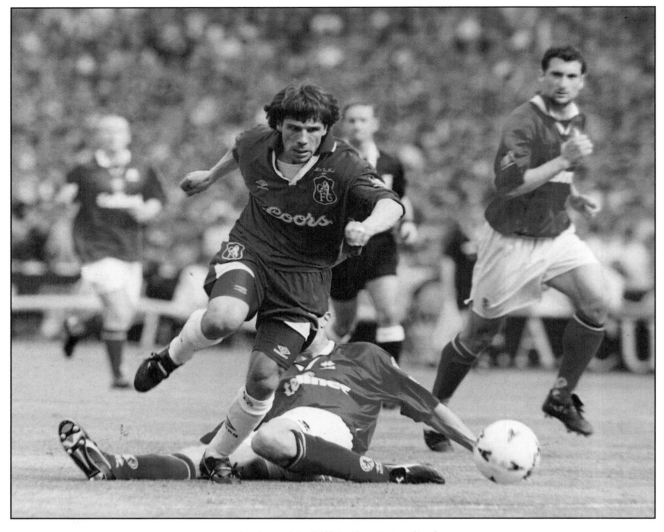

Zola shows his skill in the FA Cup final

typical modesty and sincerity. "I always believed in my ability and skill and I thought I'd need time to get to know English football. My team mates have been a big help, and step by step I've become more confident. I'm a different person now I'm here in England, more relaxed."

The reaction of the Chelsea fans, not to mention the drooling press, surely must have gone some way to making the newcomer feel at home. But his performances on the

It didn't take long for Zola settle with his Chelsea team mates, who quickly foisted upon him the nickname "Fonzie" owing to his similarity to the Happy Days star. And these, lest we forget, feature the irrepressible Dennis Wise, whose first task when confronted with Roberto Di Matteo was to tell the jovial Italian that "•••• Off" was a suitable English greeting. Di Matteo promptly signing his name with the 'welcome' in a young fan's autograph book on the

"I've always believed in my ability and skill"

pitch and the way he fitted the home game surely led to an easier transition, both for Zola and wife Franca and children Andrea and Martina.

"We have settled down very quickly, which has really helped me to concentrate on my football," announced Zola, who adapted to life at Chelsea far quicker than LeBeouf, Di Matteo and Vialli. "I'm very happy here, I feel like I've found myself again."

first day of the season (cue press "outrage"). Zola's take on the Chelsea captain?

"I get depressed when I walk into the dressing room and can't understand a word Dennis Wise is saying," he smiles. "It helps if I don't spend too much time with him, he is a bad teacher."

Zola's cheer in his new found home has been evident to anyone who has watched the delight in which he celebrates

Wembley joy for Gianfranco and Roberto Di Matteo

In his now familiar pose...

a Chelsea goal, regardless of who has scored it, and he went so far as to profess to being "sad" because Chelsea had not won a home game (in fact they'd drawn).

The eagerness to do well, and which took him to winning the Football Writers' Footballer Of The Year in his first season, clearly rubbed off on his team mate Mark Hughes, who found himself coming in third in the very same awards (and no Chelsea fan can remember when a Chelsea player last featured, let alone have two in the top three!), and rejuvenated, finished the club's top scorer last season.

"Because of the quality I've continued to learn about the game," said Sparky, paying tribute to his small team mate. "It's never too late to learn from a player like Zola."

Less happy was fellow striker Gianluca Vialli, who increasingly found himself on the substitute's bench as the Zola/Hughes partnership continued to bear fruit. It was the result of much press debate as to a rift between Vialli and Gullit, with Vialli's departure alwaysseemingly just around the corner.

"The two of them are very intelligent people," commented Zola on a situation of which he had, in effect, been the main catalyst. "They keep whatever problems they have between the two of them to themselves and we don't detect an atmosphere or tension in the changing room."

The end result of this supposed feud is that Vialli remains a Chelsea player for the forthcoming season, despite interest from Celtic, and he captured the hearts of the Chelsea faithful with the dignified manner in which he accepted his Chelsea situation, his comments on Cup Final day all about team support and victory says more than any speculative headline ever could. He did, of course, get his wish for five minutes of play on the big day.

But Chelsea's season was not about supposed rifts, or of who was leaving the club. It was about the way a small Sardinian helped raise the tempo of his club (and the play of his much larger on-field partner whom he delightfully refers to as "Hughses"), taking them to levels that Chelsea fans had been dreaming of for years.

Zola
Gola

Although it took Gianfranco Zola four matches in the Premiership to net his first goal for Chelsea, his impact had already been felt in other areas on the pitch and his rich and unselfish approach to the game noted. It wasn't long before the rewards which came with them were flooding his way.

What was perhaps even more apparent was that, unlike many noted goalscorers, there were two facets of Zola's play that truly set him apart in the Premiership. The majority of the goals that Zola scored for Chelsea in his first season were memorable pieces of football in their own right. And that the impact Zola had on many games was not restricted to simply the goal he might score, like so many

strikers we have seen before. Zola's impact on the game centred more on the fact that he alone could inspire his team with the slightest of touches, with one flick of the ball, a turn this way or that. It is so noticeable reflecting on the past season that Gianfranco Zola was not just intent on claiming personal glory, but working hard for his entire team. And in almost every game that he scored in you can guarantee that there was something else that helped Chelsea onwards in their Premiership efforts.

These, however, are the goals that helped Gianfranco Zola to become Chelsea Football Club's Player of the Year, and make an indelible impression on the club and its recent history.

Zola's unselfish play led to him setting up many chances for his team-mates

Zola slides on home with a cool head and clinical finish

EVERTON

December 7, 1996 (home) Score: 2—2

Zola's fourth game for Chelsea was a home match against Everton, frequently a tricky opponent for London's Blues, not least with the seemingly evergreen Neville Southall in goal. However, it didn't take long for the little Italian to make his mark in the kind of style that you might have expected if you'd followed Football Italia on Channel 4.

Chelsea were awarded a free kick some 35 yards out from the Everton goal, the ball placed roughly towards the centre of the field. Looking up into the packed box, Zola seemingly picked his spot and sent a high ball drifting over the head of everyone, and into the left hand side of goal, between a mesmerised Southall and an Everton defender clearly bamboozled by the craftiness of the attempt. A superb free kick.

And who was it that helped fellow Italian Gianluca Vialli snatch Chelsea's equaliser? Why Zola of course. Gullit sent a ball down the left to Zola, who controlled with sublime skill, nipped to the by-line and sent in a perfect cross for Vialli to head home. Vialli then blasted over with minutes to go, missing the chance of a precious three points.

WEST HAM

December 21, 1996 (h) Score 3—1

After a shocking performance at Sunderland which had seen Chelsea lose 3—0, many of the imports not looking at

all happy with the inclement conditions, Chelsea re-found their form against West Ham (again, never the easiest of opponents), and Zola was once more in the thick of the action.

Craig Burley sent Dan Petrescu down the right, and his cross was flicked on to the on rushing Mark Hughes thanks to a deft little back heel from Zola, Hughes picking his spot with ease.

But it was Zola's effort (Chelsea's second) that had the tabloids squealing with delight. Hughes picked up the ball in the Chelsea half and sent a perfect through ball for Zola to latch onto. Off he set down the right hand side, under the attention of the fearsome Julian Dicks. However, not only did little Zola hold off the on rushing defender, but cut inside him, and when Dicks doubled back for another go, the impish forward deftly flicked the ball past him to the right, before rifling a shot past the hapless Miklosko into the bottom left hand corner.

"Everybody loves him," said Gullit afterwards, swelling with the kind of pride a father would for his own son. "I think he stole their hearts." Probably not that of Dicks however, who had been made to look a complete fool.

ASTON VILLA

December 26, 1996 (away) Score 2—0

Chelsea's good form over the Yuletide period continued with a fine away win at Villa Park, once more powered by

His goals helped Parma to the Italian Cup and a Cup Winners' Cup final place

Zola, who bagged both the goals in a one sided contest that ended Villa's five match unbeaten run.

Zola had already had one shot saved by Mark Bosnich after Craig Burley had sent him scampering off down the right, but in the second half Zola hit the mark. Petrescu set up the Italian on the right edge of Villa's box. He nipped past one defender and his long-range shot was slightly deflected past the fumbling Bosnich.

Three minutes later Zola sealed it when Di Matteo sent a high ball from Chelsea's half into the Villa area. Fernando Nelson flunked his back header and before Bosnich could reach the ball, in had nipped the wily Zola, slotting the ball into an empty net from an awkward angle, before setting off, arms aloft, grinning from ear to ear.

SHEFFIELD WEDNESDAY

December 28, 1996 (home) Score 2–2

Despite the setback of once more conceding yet another two points at Stamford Bridge, it was left to Gianfranco Zola to set the game alight. Terry Phelan, making one of his last appearances in a Chelsea shirt, was on one of his strident dashes down the left before sliding the ball through to Mark Hughes. His pulled back cross was straight into the path of Zola, approaching from the right, who calmly slotted the ball into the back of the net. Zola was also involved in Chelsea's second. Di Matteo sent him off down the right, straight out of the Chelsea area. Approaching the Wednesday area, it took

one little look up from Zola to see Hughes rushing in, and in came an inch perfect cross for Hughes to power home with his head. A great goal made by superb control from the Italian, giving a display of his perfect first touch.

WEST BROMWICH ALBION

January 4, 1997, (home – FA Cup third round) 3–0

Running in on the back of a revenge win against Liverpool, Chelsea overcame their third round opponents (often such a tricky task for the London club) with ease. Goals from Dennis Wise and Craig Burley had made it comfortable, but giving his all to the end, Zola stole in for a third with a minute to go. A shot from Gianluca Vialli struck the right hand post of the WBA goal, and, much like his goal against Sheffield Wednesday, in came Zola to hit home from close range, with a display of cool finishing.

LIVERPOOL

January 26, 1997 (home – FA Cup fourth round) 4–2

With Chelsea 2–0 down to an impressive-looking Liverpool side, revenge was looking to be back on the boot of the Scousers, with perhaps an outside chance of Chelsea snatching a draw. Then on came Mark Hughes as substitute after half time to rekindle his developing partnership with Zola and inspire one of the most remarkable comebacks in FA Cup history.

Hughes had fired Chelsea's first before Petrescu, working

In Italy, Zola learned to take his chances – you don't get too many in Serie A

Practice, practice — and when the chances come on the pitch you'll take them...

his way through to the left of the Liverpool area was blocked. Unluckily for Liverpool, the ball ran to Hughes, who held it up as only he can, laying it back for Zola outside the area. With just one glance and one touch, the Sardinian unleashed a 25 yard drive, curling away from the outstretched figure of the imposing David James and inside the right hand post. A truly world class goal.

Yet if that wasn't enough, Zola's free kick expertise helped finish off a shell shocked Liverpool side, after he'd had a hand in Chelsea's third goal. Whipping in a free kick from the right, in nipped Vialli past a stunned Liverpool defence to head home his second, Chelsea's fourth and the match winner. The stuff of dreams.

MANCHESTER UNITED

February 22, 1997 (home) score 1—1

It didn't take long for Zola to have an impact on a game that saw the league leaders looking to exact revenge for Chelsea's earlier victory at Old Trafford, prior to Zola's arrival. But the Italian clearly had other ideas. Collecting a ball from Petrescu (again! How effective this unsung hero was for Chelsea last season) inside of Dennis Irwin, Zola nipped to the line, cutting back inside the normally solidly reliable defender, past an unsettled Gary Pallister who looked on agog as Zola wrong footed Peter Schmiechel, smashing in a fierce shot between keeper and near post, before celebrating in his usual delightful manner.

Smartly dressed and
ready for action at the
Cup Final

This classic was even chosen by BBC's *Match Of The Day* as Goal of the Month, not bad when you consider their habit of normally ignoring any Chelsea effort of note!

PORTSMOUTH

March 3, 1997 (away — FA Cup fifth round) score 4—1

Mark Hughes had given Chelsea a dream start on a foggy day on the south coast with a stupendous strike in the first half before his wily striking partner got in on the act, although at first as mere provider. It was Zola's delightful 25 yard free kick that set up Steve Clarke's powering header that would have signalled the Scots' defenders first goal for Chelsea in aeons had Dennis Wise not nipped in to poke the ball over the very line it was rapidly approaching.

Zola's next move was to collect a ball from Di Matteo from the right, who in turn had been set up by a nice cut from Hughes, and with Zola placed centrally, it didn't take much for the Italian to plant the ball straight into the back of the Portsmouth net for Chelsea's third goal of the day.

SUNDERLAND

March 16, 1997 (home) Score 6—2

What better way to avenge Chelsea's 3—0 defeat at Roker Park than to simply decimate the opposition with the nation watching on TV with the awesome ease with which Chelsea finished off Sunderland at Stamford Bridge.

And typically it was Gianfranco Zola that set the ball rolling. After some exemplary work from Dan Petrescu in the Sunderland area, the Romanian set up Zola who fired in a spectacular volley past French goalkeeper Lionel Perez in a move that reeked of international class.

And it was a Zola cross that set up Frank Sinclair's fluke of a header that inadvertently bounced over the head of the hapless keeper for Chelsea's second, whilst a cracking Zola shot later in the game from a Di Matteo pass could only be parried by Perez before Dan Petrescu added his name to the score sheet.

SOUTHAMPTON

March 19, 1997 (home) score 1—0

The last game in which Chelsea would triumph before a disastrous slump in form threatened their FA Cup ambitions saw the Blues victorious against Southampton, their protagonists on the opening day of the season.

A typically dour affair was brightened by, who else, Zola. Mark Hughes, indulging in his usual ball holding expertise, set up the Sardinian 30 yards out from the Saints goal. Zola barely looked up before he drove a scorching shot past the keeper and into the back of the Southampton net.

Another fine example of how these two fine forwards complement each other.

Zola proved his worth for Parma

WIMBLEDON

April 13, 1997 (Highbury — FA Cup semi-final) Score 3—0

Typically, Zola saved his very best for the last game he would score in for Chelsea in the 1996—7 season. This was Chelsea's second FA Cup semi final in consecutive years, and following on the back of a poor run of form, the typically ebullient Wimbledon were fancied for a bit of an upset.

But buoyed by their victories over Liverpool and Portsmouth, and graced with the kind of luck a team needs to win the Cup in their match with Leicester, Chelsea had other ideas.

Hughes had put Chelsea ahead after a tense opening half hour, following good work from Zola on the left, but after the break Gianfranco really turned on the style. Roberto Di Matteo picked up the ball about 35 yards out from the Wimbledon goal. Hi through ball to Zola saw the little Italian darting to his left before flicking the ball back right, and, out turning Dean Blackwell he pushes the ball further away from the hapless defender, before blasting a shot past Neil Sullivan and sending Chelsea further towards their second FA Cup Final in four years.

The Ruud Revolution

Ruud Gullit tasted managerial success before the 1996–7 season had even begun. Not in his astute acquisitions throughout the summer, but when Chelsea won the Umbro Tournament for the second time at Nottingham Forest, defeating Ajax in the final. As a pre-season tournament, it has little bearing on the season ahead, but offers a reasonable indication of how well new players are going to adapt to the rigours of the Premiership. But retaining the trophy at Everton's Goodison Park prior to the new season in such emphatic style: a victory over Newcastle on penalties, with new Dutch goal-keeper Ed De Goey making three impressive saves, and a thorough 3–1 defeat of home side Everton in the final with two goals from Gianfranco Zola, suggests that Gullit's side is on the verge of the breakthrough that Chelsea fans have waited so long for. To challenge for the title.

A run in the FA Cup that took the Blues to Wembley for the second time in four years finally saw Dennis Wise go up to lift the silverware that players, directors and fans alike had waited so long for. After Chelsea's decimation of a Wimbledon team many thought capable of upsetting the favourites in the semi-final, with Zola inspired in scoring his team's second goal, Chelsea took on Bryan Robson's relegated Middlesbrough in the Final. Billed by the press as the Azzuri of Stamford Bridge taking on the samba dancing Brazilians of the northern club, the diminutive figure of

Chelsea are finally on
the verge of a strong
title challenge

Jump to it: the England wall attempts to stop the little man's free-kick at Wembley

Gareth Southgate gets to grips with Zola at Wembley

Zola was pitched against the equally vertically-challenged Juninho as being the prime movers in the game. But assumption is often the mother of all mistakes, and in the end it was Zola's fellow countryman Roberto Di Matteo who stole the limelight with a glorious strike (the quickest ever in a Cup Final). His 42nd-second goal, a viciously dipping 35 yard shot that gave goalkeeper Ben Roberts no chance whatsoever, in effect killed off a game which gave Middlesbrough their final shot at glory in a season that had also seen them fall to Leicester City in the Coca-Cola Cup. But although Juninho ran his heart out in his final appearance for Boro to no avail, Gianfranco Zola still had something to add. When Eddie Newton set up another Chelsea attack late in the second half, he slipped the ball out to Dan Petrescu whose delicate chip over the Boro defence seemed destined to go out until the tiny Sardinian darted forward and with the most remarkable foresight, backheeled the ball back across the face of the goal and directly into the path of Eddie Newton who fired home, securing Chelsea's

cup victory. It was a delightful touch, displaying the fact that although he could be quiet throughout a game, Zola still had the ability, as Gullit so rightly pointed out when buying the player, to turn the course of a match with just one touch, thanks to his supreme awareness.

The delight from the Chelsea players was more than evident in their post match celebrations, which continued on the Wembley turf for an unprecedented 45 minutes. Norwegian goalkeeper Frode Grodas resplendent in his Viking hat, Roberto Di Matteo with a Chelsea scarf as a headband, Frank Sinclair and Eddie Newton singing away their bitter disappointment of four years previous, and Gianfranco Zola, with a massive "Z" atop his head, grinning from ear to ear and kissing his prized winner's medal in delight.

So where did Chelsea go from here? Would Ruud Gullit sign a new contract? Would Mark Hughes? Would Vialli, who got his desired five minute run out in the Final, be off? The press hysteria that greets any comment, no matter

Some of the techniques
honed in Serie A are
being taken on board
in West London

Zola will remain central to
Maldini's plans for the
World Cup

Skipping past the defenders like they're not there...

how out of context, turning it into panic inducing headlines worked hard on the Chelsea team. When Zola himself announced that he would like to finish his playing career in his native country (a fair wish by any standards), the headlines screamed that he was off, quitting the very team he'd been professing his love for days earlier.

"The thing I'm sure of is that I'll remain in London next year," said Zola, declaring an intent to see out his contract with Chelsea ignored by the press. "I'm no longer a little boy and I want to finish my career in Italy," he added, in a move which prompted the scaremongering.

As it is, Zola retains his Number 25 shirt for the forthcoming 1997–8 season, and his form in Chelsea's pre-season friendlies impressive, leading to the two excellent strikes against Everton in the Umbro tournament. Alongside him, Gianluca Vialli, resplendent in his No. 9 shirt, firing home Chelsea's first goal against The Toffees and giving Ruud Gullit (contract signed) something to think about for the forthcoming season. And joining them, a host of new signings that have had the press and pundits pontificating on the pros and cons of overseas players, of the Bosman ruling and of the development of homegrown players.

It's a melee of arguments that frequently features Ruud Gullit and his policy of not paying the daft prices requested for homegrown players, but scouring the clubs of Europe and acquiring the likes of Zola. Yet given the cut and thrust nature of the world of football, it is only those teams that buy wisely that will endeavour to make headway. One only has to look at the troubles that befell Bryan Robson at Middlesbrough with first Branco, then Emerson and seemingly always Fabrizio Ravanelli to see that things can go wrong.

Not so for Ruud Gullit, whose main problem, apart from having to deal with constant press sniping, was what to do with a player of Gianluca Vialli's calibre when Gianfranco Zola and Mark Hughes were combining so well up front. Gullit's purchases of last season have all settled well into his integrated, European style squad system (a system also deployed at Arsenal to good effect). His buying over the recent summer has seen him shore up Chelsea's leaky defence with Nigerian Celestine Babayaro and Frenchman

Gianfranco Zola:
Chelsea's maestro

Bernard Lambourde, deal with last season's goalkeeping crises by signing Dutch international Ed De Goey, and add Uruguayan Gustavo Poyet to the midfield and strengthen the attack with Norwegian Tore Andre Flo. And all for less cost than one Alan Shearer.

The selling of Craig Burley to Celtic did signify that some players were unable to deal with the new system.

"I only want players who want to stay," says the Chelsea boss. "Some players had problems with the new regime, others moaned at the start, got in the team and took advantage of that to get a transfer. There has been a lot of discussion about my signings, but the supporters aren't complaining and there is no feeling here that there's some sort of difference between the British and foreign players. Other clubs might have a problem with their foreign players because maybe they are not doing so well. At Chelsea we all speak English, go out together, play golf together. We are not like a lot of strangers."

Despite the likes of Paul Parker (signed as a stop gap defender last season) suggesting, possibly with some dis-content as the club had let him go, in the press that Gullit would indeed like to win the Premiership without having to field a homegrown player, Gullit's claims of unity are backed up by Scottish defender Steve Clarke, playing the best football of his career under the Dutchman's unique guidance.

"There's a good spirit among the lads and everyone shares in the jokes and the banter."

With a squad that also features British youngsters like Jody Morris, Mark Nicholls, Neil Clemence and Paul Hughes alongside the noted and celebrated internationals, the good spirit that pervades the Stamford Bridge dressing room has seen Chelsea move from being nearly rans to Cup Winners who will represent England on the international stage in the European Cup Winners Cup (for which they are clear favourites) and mount a serious challenge for Manchester United's title.

And with the Football Writer's Player of the Year Gianfranco Zola raring to go in the starting line-up, the Blues look like more than a dark horse in the increasingly open race for the Premiership title.